100 Things for My Child

Sam Sloane

Copyright © 2024 Sam Sloane

All rights reserved.

No part of this book may be reproduced or used in any manner without the prior written permission of the copyright owner, except for the use of brief quotations in a book review.

To request permissions, contact the publisher at ssermas@typingmonkeypublishers.com.

ISBN 979-8-9876600-4-1

Cover Design by Kimberly Platt
Layout by Stephanie Sermas

Published by
Typing Monkey Publishers, LLC

www.typingmonkeypublishers.com

The following is a list of things which I found to have helped me be a good member of the human race. As every person on this planet has, I have faced wonders, delights, tragedies and sorrows. My most profound moments were those when I could take time to reflect on what it is to be content. Happiness is a mercurial and often elusive idea for me. But I can understand contentment. It is when I feel connected when alone, strong when challenged, kind when hurting and purposeful when lost. You have brought a light, innocence and vulnerability into my world I could never have imagined as a younger person. For this, I am forever grateful.   I love you, my child.

1.

Learn and wield the power of the word "why?"

2.

Eat well. Learn to love food.

3.

Learn to cook good, simple dishes that you love to eat and share.

4.

Teach yourself how to use a knife like a chef.

5.

Explore the world's cuisines.   The quickest path to connection with another is through the food they love.

6.

Be the first to offer help at a dinner gathering or party.

7.

When you wake up, hug someone you love.
If alone, hug yourself.

8.

Stay current on what's happening in sports.
Always a great way to connect with others
across the street, country and globe.

9.

Be a good winner and better loser.

10.

Place yourself in nature often. Not just on perfect days, but on rainy, windy, cold and hot ones. You will be amazed at what you see.

11.

Know a path or trail inside and out - the trees, plants, flowers, sounds and features.

12.

If you can't sleep, get up and do something.

13.

Leave the day even slightly better than you found it.

14.

Smile at strangers.

15.

Be the first to say hello.

16.

Eat fresh snow.

17.

If you are feeling low, call someone and ask how they are doing.

18.

Write letters - even a short note can bring great peace to another.

19.

Learn three toasts: one to celebrate, one to remember and one to thank.

20.

Love the world's cities.

21.

Select our family history to pass on.

22.

Wherever you live, become an expert on the greatest things about it and help others see the beautiful things there.

23.

Pizza.

24.

Ask for help. The four most powerful words
I know in human connection have been
"I need your help."

25.

Be kind to animals, even the weird ones.

26.

Swim in the ocean annually.

27.

Vote - at all levels. This is a tremendous and important part of who we are and how we can be a part of the world in which we live.

28.

Welcome Mondays with open arms.

29.

Make your bed.

30.

When asked to do something by your grandmother, do it quickly and with care.

31.

Same for your mother.

32.

Laugh at stupid things like we do.

33.

Love is free and more potent the more you give away.

34.

Meditate - start small for a few minutes each day and work your way up.

35.

Share your favorite candy with someone.

36.

When you meet someone to love and share your life, care for them more than anything in the world.

37.

Capture the exciting moments to reflect back when things aren't as new and fresh.

38.

Cry when you want and don't hold back.

39.

I know you love music as much as I do. Explore the new, the old, the esoteric and the familiar.

40.

You have every right as a human to be mad, sad, frustrated, confused and lost.

41.

You will feel loss, pain, sorrow, rage and shame. Embrace and examine these feelings. With them you can then know joy, satiety, fulfillment and profundity.

42.

Understand and study the world's major religions. We are guided by order and regularity. If only the world we live in were so structured.

43.

Keep running barefoot in the rain on the sand.

44.

Pancakes.

45.

Try to read 20 books a year.

46.

Find ten of your favorite books and share them with friends, strangers, loves and family.

47.

Keep healthy. You have the gift of a good physical body. Be able to walk long distances, run fast, bicycle, swim and climb.

48.

Eat breakfast. And second breakfast, if you like.

49.

As you find things you like, write them down.

50.

Keep collections.

51.

Save your money. You'll need it when you least expect it.

52.

Love your mother with your whole heart.   She is strong and fierce and loves you above all else.

53.

You are the light in your grandmother's eyes and heart. It is such an amazing relationship you have which will carry you through life. Be kind to her. Remember her stories and help her make new ones.

54.

Brush your teeth. No one likes bad breath.

55.

You are not alone.

56.

As you grow you will be faced with great experiences. Not all will be enjoyable, and you will be scared. It's okay.

57.

This, too, shall pass.

58.

Love art and museums as you have.

59.

Keep your library card ready. It's an amazing weapon.

60.

Do not hold resentments. Confront them, find the cause and, if possible, clear them through amends.

61.

Dance any old way you want to.

62.

Have an opinion. That doesn't mean shout it from the rooftops or that others are wrong.

63.

When you have children of your own give them time. The gifts and experiences are good, but as we get older, we remember the time spent together.

64.

Remember your grandmother and grandfather (from whom we get our name). They lived in a large world from a very small place.

65.

Stop at roadside monuments
and places of interest.

66.

Skip the Interstate.

67.

Keep drawing. You are an artist and have raw talent and great instruction.

68.

Always have a joke or two.

69.

Enjoy movies, watch the ones that make you laugh and the ones that make you think. Learn from actors who you admire.

70.

Pack lightly, but with thought.

71.

When you give a gift, give it freely with a whole heart.

72.

Say yes to new experiences, even when you don't want to.

73.

Don't be afraid to say no.

74.

Follow the path of others who have endured hardships and joy.

75.

Learn always.

76.

Love technology. Use it and master it.
It will help you leave it behind when you can.

77.

Smile at the sky, the rain and the heat.

78.

Dip your fingers in wax from a melted candle.
It feels so weird and cool at the same time.

79.

Be you and always you.

80.

Have several good stories about something you know or have done.

81.

Leave change for smaller kids to find.
It's an amazing sight to see.

82.

Semicolons have always been a favorite tool of mine; use them wisely.

83.

Give blood if you are able. One day a person's life will depend on it.

84.

Eat bread warm from the oven. No shame in enjoying one of the greatest pleasures ever, even parked in the car outside the bakery.

85.

Embrace the dark.
Your eyes and mind will adjust.

86.

Learn the constellations and teach someone else.
They are the guides we have used to navigate
and to explain and wonder.

87.

Keep a personal dictionary. I still have my father's and his father's.

88.

Words are important.

89.

If you are in the wrong, quickly acknowledge,
apologize and make amends.
It's a hard thing to do.

90.

When you lie to others you are chipping off pieces of yourself and throwing them away.

91.

_____ is one of your greatest friends, allies and advocates. They will help you and love you unconditionally.

92.

Find a mentor and learn from their path. You will share a special bond through life, and they will need you as much as you will need them.

93.

As you grow older, enjoy the past but don't let it own you.

94.

Use all your senses when hiking or walking in nature. You will hear and feel and smell things beyond what your eyes see.

95.

Learn spices and herbs. The finest cuisines across the globe use them beautifully and sublimely to create memory, experience and home for billions of people.

96.

Become a good card shuffler. It feels good.

97.

Practice reading upside down and backwards; there is a lot to learn from things not right in front of us.

98.

Be relentless in your curiosity.

99.

Stay in bed all day once in a while.

100.

Keep adding to this list!

Things I hope we will do together:

Climb enchanted rock every year
Take the trans-Siberian railway
Hike the Appalachian trail
Sail In Maine
Sleep under the stars on a beach
Build more LEGOs
Write our own book about the best pancakes in the world
Run
Have you beat me in a race
Talk daily
Make our video game
Sing bad Christmas Carols
Eat too much cereal at 3 am
Cry, laugh and smile at the world
Hold hands as we have

You are my sun, moon and stars.   I learn more about patience, kindness, love and contentment from our time than you may ever know.

I love you.

www.ingramcontent.com/pod-product-compliance
Lightning Source LLC
Chambersburg PA
CBHW041217130526
44582CB00026BA/57